BOURNEMOUTH TO EVERCREECH JUNCTION

Vic Mitchell and Keith Smith

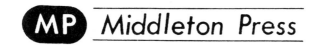
MP *Middleton Press*

Cover picture: Designed by the LMS and built by BR, class 2 2–6–2T no. 41242 accelerates away from the rural station at Cole, with the 9.45am Highbridge to Templecombe service on 27th October 1962. (C.L. Caddy)

Design – Deborah Goodridge

First published November 1987
ISBN 0 906520 46 0

© *Middleton Press, 1987*

Typeset by CitySet - Bosham 573270

Published by Middleton Press
Easebourne Lane
Midhurst, West Sussex
GU29 9AZ
☎ 073 081 3169

Printed & bound by Biddles Ltd,
Guildford and Kings Lynn

CONTENTS

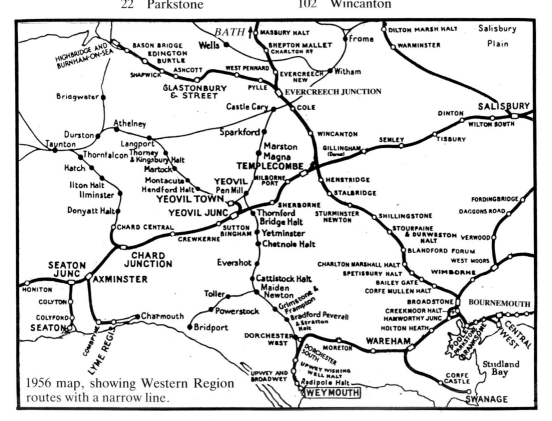

1956 map, showing Western Region routes with a narrow line.

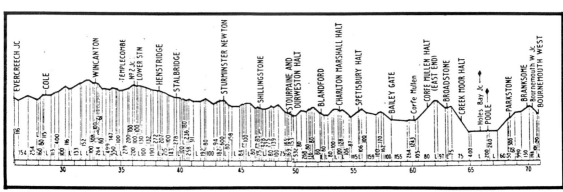

Gradient profile. Mileages are from Bath.

ACKNOWLEDGEMENTS

We are very grateful for the help received from the photographers mentioned in the caption credits and also for the assistance given by Dr. J.A. Boudreau, K. Brown, Dr. P.E. Catermole (Somerset & Dorset Railway Trust Museum), R.T.S. Dagger, Mr. & Mrs. Drew, J.R. Fairman, C. Hooper, N.H. Pankhurst, R. Randell, R. Resch, E. Staff, N. Stanyon, A. Ward and our ever helpful wives.

INTRODUCTION

This album is intended to be the first of a trilogy centred on the hub of the old Somerset & Dorset Railway empire at Evercreech Junction. It takes followers of our South Coast Railway Series inland to enjoy the beauty of the Dorset countryside and the unique charm of the S&D. The interesting southern arm of the system often receives less attention than the spectacular northern part and so we have attempted to portray some of the less known details of this section and the countryside it served.

We have selected material from the less commonly used sources and have thus attempted to give readers a fresh look at the line and its traffic. We believe that almost all the views contained herein have not been previously published in books on the S&D.

The station maps are to the scale of 25″ to 1 mile and the population figures quoted apply at the time of closure of the line.

GEOGRAPHICAL SETTING

From Bournemouth to Broadstone the route crosses a westward extension of the infertile sands and gravels of the New Forest. Prior to urbanisation, these bore extensive pine woods which were the inspiration for the name of the famous express.

A steep descent from Parkstone takes the line to near sea level as it crosses Parkstone Bay on an embankment. After passing through the ancient maritime town of Poole, the track skirts Holes Bay before regaining the sandy heights at Broadstone.

The Corfe Mullen spur reached about 200ft above sea level before descending to the Stour Valley. The railway ran in the Stour Gap, which breaches the chalk ridge extending from Salisbury Plain to beyond Dor-chester. After crossing bands of Kimmeridge and Gault Clay near Shillingstone, the route passed through a Corallian Limestone ridge at Sturminster Newton.

The line entered Blackmoor Vale and followed the valley of the River Cale, a tributary of the Stour, as far as Wincanton. North of this town, the route reached a summit, crossed the watershed and descended to eventually meet the west-flowing River Brue. The limestone in this region is a southern extension of the Cotswolds.

Evercreech Junction was situated at the eastern end of the relatively level part of Somerset, at the southern extremity of the Mendip Hills.

HISTORICAL BACKGROUND

The first passenger railway in Dorset was the London & South Western Railway's Southampton to Dorchester line, which took a circuitous route via Ringwood and Wimborne. It was known as "Castleman's Corkscrew", after a solicitor in the latter town who had been its principal promoter, and came into use on 1st June 1847. A branch to Poole Harbour (now the Hamworthy goods line) was provided for passengers to Poole and the then small village of Bournemouth. The Dorset Central Railway's branch from Wimborne to Blandford (St. Mary) was opened on 1st November 1860 and was operated by the LSWR until August 1863.

The Somerset Central Railway commenced operation on 28th August 1854 with a line from Highbridge Wharf to Glastonbury, built to the broad gauge of 7 feet. This line reached Templecombe on 3rd February 1862, the year in which the two companies amalgamated to form the Somerset & Dorset Railway. Physical union took place at Cole (then Bruton) on 31st August 1863, when the line north from Blandford was opened. Broad gauge track was provided south to Cole, this later being converted to standard 4′ 8½″.

The LSWR opened a branch from its Wimborne–Dorchester line to Poole on 2nd December 1872. This was extended to the expanding town of Bournemouth on 15th June 1874, terminating at a station later known as Bournemouth West. The connection to East (later Central) station followed in 1888.

Through running between Bournemouth and Bath became possible with the opening of the S&D's Bath extension from Evercreech Junction on 20th July 1874. An unsatisfactory feature of this service was the need for reversal at Wimborne. To obviate this, a spur between Broadstone and Corfe Mullen was opened; to goods trains on 14th December 1885 and to passengers on 1st November 1886. This completed the railway network of the area.

In 1866 the S&DR was declared bankrupt. By 1875, after nine years in receivership, the company was financially exhausted and arrangements were made for the London &

South Western Railway to lease it jointly with the Midland Railway. Thus the S&DJR was born and the leasing companies had the benefit of direct access to business remote from their own areas. This included the Somerset coalfield and the Bristol Channel ferry services from Burnham.

From 1st July 1923, the recently formed SR and LMSR became joint *owners* of the route between Bath and Broadstone. It continued to be operated as a separate railway until 1st July 1930, when the distinctive Prussian blue trains were replaced by SR green coaches and LMS-liveried locomotives. The SR took responsibility for permanent way and signalling while the LMS took over operation of the line.

An endless muddle followed nationalisation in 1948. Initially the London Midland Region continued to operate the line from Bath, traffic supervision being from Southampton! In 1950, the Western Region took control of the line north from Cole (commercially) while the Southern Region operated the line with locomotives loaned by the LMR. Further rearrangements in 1958 gave the WR complete control south to Henstridge, except that Templecombe remained in the SR. In January 1963, lines west of Salisbury were transferred to the WR and the regional boundary was moved to a point south of Shillingstone.

Through passenger trains north of Bath ceased to operate in September 1962, long distance goods trains having been re-routed in 1959. Withdrawal of all passenger services took place on 7th March 1966 but freight continued to be carried south from Blandford Forum until 6th January 1969.

Wimborne's original link with the S&D lost its passenger service on 11th July 1920, but milk trains continued to use the line until 17th June 1933. Wimborne lost its remaining passenger service on 4th May 1964 but retained a goods line via Broadstone until 2nd May 1977.

Thus only the Branksome–Poole part of the route is in use today and electrification of it (and the line to Weymouth) is being carried out at the time of writing.

PASSENGER SERVICES

The initial service north of Templecombe was one of five weekday and two Sunday trains each way and upon extension southwards four and two, respectively, were provided, running between Burnham and Poole.

With the opening of the Evercreech Junction–Bath route in 1874, a service of four return journeys between Bournemouth and Bath was operated, with most Burnham trains thereafter not running south of Templecombe. No trains were run on Sundays. A decade later, there were six trains each way, on weekdays only, and this service had been increased to seven by 1894. There were also several local journeys south of Templecombe. Some of these continued to run via Wimborne until 1920.

Through trains or coaches were a feature of the timetables until 1962. Common destinations included Liverpool, Manchester, Newcastle and Sheffield, while Lincoln, Nottingham, Cleethorpes, Bradford, Burnham and Bristol were amongst places served from time to time. Occasionally services from the North joined the LSWR main line at Templecombe to reach Sidmouth, Exmouth or Plymouth for example.

The opulent Edwardian era saw the start of two through trains to the South Coast from Manchester in 1910. The "Sunny South Express" ran to East Sussex and the other to Bournemouth via the SDJR. This train remained un-named until 1927, when it became the "Pines Express". It ran every weekday throughout the year until 8th September 1962, except for the 1939–49 period of war and austerity.

A summary of the basic service in the inter-war years would show 4 fast and 4 slow trains Bath–Bournemouth and 4 slow trains south of Templecombe. The post WWII corresponding figures would show 2, 3 and 3, for most years, except for the last two when "The Pines" had been withdrawn. There were a few additional trains north of Templecombe (from Burnham branch) and extra services south of Broadstone, all of which will be mentioned in future albums.

Services should have ceased on 3rd January 1966 but continued until closure on 7th March of that year, due to problems with the licensees of the replacement buses. During this period, four trains each way were provided, all running through to Bath.

Two notable features of passenger services on the route were the large number of additional through services run for holiday makers on summer Saturdays and the paucity of trains on Sundays. These were limited to local milk trains to which a few coaches were attached and to excursion trains, some of which ran on a regular basis for a few summers.

Up trains at intermediate S&D stations

	1910	1924	1938	1948	1965
Bailey Gate	7	7	9	7	7
Spetisbury	5	6	8	6	–
Blandford	10	12	15	14	8
Shillingstone	6	8	9	7	7
Sturminster	9	8	10	8	8
Stalbridge	6	9	9	10	8
Henstridge	6	5	7	6	7
Wincanton	12	10	10	12	10
Cole	9	10	7	10	10

THROUGH TRAINS
LIVERPOOL and MANCHESTER
TO
BOURNEMOUTH WEST, via Bath.

Week Days only.

	a.m.	a.m.	a.m.	a.m.	a.m.	a.m.	a.m.	a.m.	a.m.	a.m.	a.m.	a.m.	a.m.	a.m.	p.m.		p.m.	p.m.
			SO		SO	R					SO					September 2nd.		
							RT		R R	SX C Y			R		R		Q	J
Bradford (Frstr Sq.) dep.	1 38			7 55	7 35	7 45	7 45			10 25	1025	1058		12 32			8m25	8 55
Harrogate .... "				6 50	6 50	6 50	6 50			9 28	9 28	1030		12 9			8 m 7	8 7
Leeds (City) .... "	3 10			8 10	8 10	8 20	8 20			1052	1052	1130		1 0			9 m 2	9m22
York .... "	2 5			7 28	7 28	7 28	7 28			1020	1020	1020		12 13			8m10	8 10
Sheffield .... "	4 42		6 20	9 20	9 20	9 20	9 20			1147	1147	1242		2 3			10m23	10m50
Chesterfield .... "	5 13		6 54	9 45	9 45	9 55	9 47			1148	1147	1 7		2 24			11m23	11r24
Liverpool (Lime St.) dep.							9 40	9 40					12 y 0		10 0			
Burnley { Bank Top "							8 k 5						10k14		MA19			
{ Barracks "							8 k 9						10k19		8A15			
Accrington .... "						6•42	8k23						10k34		8A56			
Blackburn .... "						6•46	8•612			8•35	8•39		10k47		8A56			
Bolton (Trinity St.) "						7•11	8•58			9 j 9	j 1		11k17		9A30			
Manchester { Cen. "						6•48	10d40			9 45	9 45		12 20		10 15			
{ L. Rd. "						8 55	9 20			10 10	1010		12,20		9A55			
{ Vic. "						8 35	8•36						11 40					
Halifax .... "						6•43	8 40						10k15		7 50			
Huddersfield .... "						7 59	9 f 6						10k25		8 5			
Rochdale .... "						7•56	9m12			9 j16	9j16		X11k29		9 7			
Oldham (Clegg St.) "						8 45	10d410			10 21	1021		12k30		10 26			
Stockport .... "						7 59	8c•25			8 32	8 32		10X10		5 30			
Blackpool (Central) "						9 24	9ee13			9 20	9 29		11X15		6 54			
Preston .... "						8 35 25	9 18			9 57	9 57		11X13		7 37			
Wigan (Nth Wstrn) "							9 18			9 43	9 43		11X15		8 43			
Birkenhead (W'dsde) "							9 55			10 20	1020		12X10		9 35			
Chester (General) .. "							10 45			1045			1 X 4		11 20			
Crewe .... "	5u10		6 55	6 55	7 46		8 30 8 25			10 40 1040			1 0		8m55	8 55		
Lincoln .... dep.				7 45			10 09 9 50			1032	2	21153		2 13			10m43	10 43
Nottingham .... "	5 5		6 30	7 55 8 32	1015	1015	10 9 1037			1 7	1240	1 25	SX10					
Leicester .... "				7 48			10 e 0			1110	12/46	1246	1 43	2 57				
Derby .... "	6 12	6 20		8 22	1024	1022	1052			1124	12/15	1215	2 0	3 12			12m5	12r37
Burton .... "	6 28	6 40		8 38		1051	11 7			1218	1/39	1 55	2 52	3 54	5 40		1 m 10	1 7
Birmingham (New St.) "	7 30	7 45	9 12	9 23	1045	1123	1248	1		1 20	1 39	2/32	3 48	4 47	6•33		2 28	2 37
Cheltenham .... arr.	8 46	8 55	10	9 1019			1248	1										
Andover Junction arr.				1 5			4 1	4 5		6 12			1016					
Salisbury .... "				2•22			5 46	5 46		7 0			1121					
Southampton { Cen. "				1•58			4 57	4 57		8 6								
{ Ter. "				2 r 6			5 5	5 5		8 38			1156					
Eastleigh .... "				2 25			5 5	5 5		7 41			11 38					
Portsm'th & St'hsea "				3 v 1			6 11	6 11		9 36			2•28					
Gloucester .... arr.	9 0	9 8	1019	1031	12 0	1227	1250 1258	1 16		1 22		2/42 3	14 0	4/58			2 42	2 52
Bath .... "	10 16	1030	1130	12 1	1255	1 27	1 50 1 50	2 10		2 15	2 36	2 48	3 56 4 56	6m24			3 52	4 5
Blandford .... "	12 17	1210								4 0	4 17	4 30	5 38 6 35	9 27				
Poole .... "	12 41	1241	1 51		2 53	4 23	3 53 5 34	10		4 24	4 41	4 56	6 3 7	1 10 0			6 27	6 55
Swanage .... "	2 40	2 40	3 25		4 23 5	25	2 5 2 15	2		5r21	5 27	6 4	7 21 8 36				8 54	8 54
Weymouth .... "	2 22	3 13	50		3 50 5	47	5 47 6 245	47		6r24		6 24	7 24 8 42				8 54	8 54
Parkstone .... "	1 31	1 72	1 2		3 23 4	84	8 4 85	14		5 14	5	14 5	6 37 7 34	10 8			6 37	8 7
Bournemouth West. "	1255	1255	2 31		3 03 5	44	54 54	22		4 37		6 37	6 16 7 13	1018			6 39	7 7

A On Aug. 12th, 19th, 26th, dep. Bolton 9k17, Blackburn 8k35, Burnley (B.T.) 8k12, Burnley (Bks.) 8k15, Accrington 8k44 p.m. On Sept. 2nd dep. Bolton 9k17, Blackburn 8k35, Burnley (B.T.) 8k12, Burnley (Bks.) 8k15. Accrington 8k44 p.m.   **AA** To Aug. 26th inclusive.   **a** On Sats. Birmingham dep. 5 45, Cheltenham arr. 6 45 p.m.   **aa** On Sats to Aug. 27th inclusive dep. Oldham 9 29 a.m.   **B** Arr 7 21 p.m. on 10th, 17th and 24th Sept.   **b** 6 30 a.m. on Sats.   **bb** Via Preston. On Sats. until Aug. 5th, leaves at 8k7 a.m.   **C** Thro Carrs., Bradford, Leeds, Lincoln, Nottingham, and Leicester to Bournemouth West.   **D** Leaves at 4 34 on Mons. and 5 0 a.m. on Sats.   **d** 3 47 p.m. on Sept. 10th.   **dd** Manchester 9 55 a.m., Stockport 10 5 a.m. on Sats.   **E** On Sats. leaves at 8k12 a.m.   **e** Not on Mons., Fris., and Sats.   **ee** Sats. excepted. On Sats. commencing Sept. 3rd, dep. Blackpool 7 50, Preston 8 55 a.m.   **f** On Sats. until Sept. 10th, leaves Derby 12 55, Burton 1 12, Birmingham 1 55, and arrives Cheltenham 2 56 and Gloucester 3 12 p.m. On Sept. 17th and 24th, leaves Nottingham 11 27, Lincoln 9 25 a.m., Derby 12 35, Burton 12 15, Birmingham 1 30, and arrives Cheltenham 2 27 and Gloucester 2 40 p.m.   **g** Dep. Liverpool (L.St.) 11 55 a.m. Sats.   **h** On Sats. Gloucester 5 4, Bath 6 45 p.m.   **J** Thro Carrs. Bradford & Leeds to Bournemouth West.   **j** Via Manchester Victoria and London Road Stations. Passengers cross the City at their own expense.   **K** Via Manchester (Victoria) & Stockport.   **M** Oldham (Mumps).   **m** applies until 2 p.m. Aug. 26th and Sept. 2nd only.   **n** Swanage 5 4 p.m., Weymouth 5 38 p.m. until Sept. 2nd.   **p** Via Preston.   **Q** Thro Express, Manchester (L. Rd.) to Bournemouth West; also Thro Carrs. from Colne, Manchester (Vic) and Liverpool (L.St.) until Aug. 5th; and Thro Carrs. Bradford and Leeds to Bournemouth West on nights of July 8th, Aug. 26th, and Sept. 2nd.   **q** Leeds 10 38, Sheffield 11 35 a.m. and Chesterfield 12 noon on Sats. Sept. 17th & 24th.   **R** Restaurant Cars are run by these trains on some parts of the journey, Bank Holidays excepted.   **r** Leaves Bradford 8 23, Leeds 9 2, Sheffield 10 25, Chesterfield 10 57, Derby 11 43, and Burton 12 5 on nights of July 15th and Aug. 19th.   **SO** or **S0** Sats. only.   **SX** or **SX** Sats. excepted.   **T** Pines Express. Thro' Carrs. Manchester (Lon. Rd.) to Bournemouth West, and Thro Carrs. Liverpool (Lime St.) to Bournemouth West and Southampton (Central and Terminus and Thro Carrs, Bradford and Leeds to Bournemouth West, Tues, Weds, and Thurs. only.   **t** Due Swanage 5 36 p.m., Weymouth 5 38 p.m. Mons. to Fris. to September 2nd; on Sats. due Swanage 5 27 p.m. & Weymouth 5 47 p.m.   **U** Blandford 12 27, Poole 12 54, Parkstone 1 17, Bournemouth West 1 7, Weymouth 2 31 p.m. Sats.   **u** Will not apply on Sats., July 9th to August 17th inclusive.   **v** Salisbury 2 14 p.m. Southampton Central 2 12 p.m.

Southampton Terminus 2 22 p.m. Portsmouth and Southsea 4 4 p.m. on Sats.   **X** On Sats. dep. Manchester (L.Rd.) 12 45 p.m., Huddersfield 10 52, Oldham 11 53, Rochdale 11 59, Halifax 10,54 a.m., Blackpool (N.) 12 5, Preston 12 12, Wigan 12 40, Crewe 2 1, Birkenhead 12 5, Chester 12 50, Stockport 12 55 p.m.   **Y** Thro Express, Bradford & Leeds to Bournemouth West.   **Z** Will not apply on Sats. Sept. 17th & 24th.   **z** Sat. nights. Sun. mrns. only.   **•** Passengers cross from Manchester (Vic.) to (Cen.) Stations at their own expense.

L.M.S. AND SOUTHERN RAILWAY COMPANIES' LUNCHEON BASKETS.

All luncheon baskets and tea trays handed to the Committee's servants by passengers, or removed from the carriages by searchers or others, must be immediately taken to the parcels office and way-billed by next train to the station marked upon them, the No. of the basket being entered on the way-bill. The baskets, etc., must be examined when taken to the parcels office, and if any of the fittings are missing, the name of the person taking the basket to the office must be registered on the way-bill.

The ordinary fittings of a luncheon basket are knife and fork, plate, bottle, glass, cork screw, napkin, and small earthenware tray.

The fittings belonging to tea trays vary according to the number tea is supplied for. Should anything appear to the guard to be missing, a report must be made on the journal to this effect.

BOURNEMOUTH WEST

1. The first station on the site had two platforms, a single-road locomotive shed and a 42ft. turntable and was opened on 15th June 1874 as the terminus of the line from Poole. A second station was added in the following year. Double track to Poole came into use on 26th October 1886 and to Bournemouth East (later Central) in 1888. Also in 1888, the two station buildings at Bournemouth West were united and extended to form the structure seen here. This postcard was franked 9 APR 14. (SDRT collection)

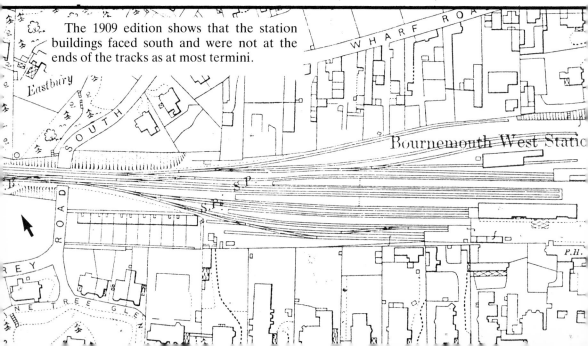

The 1909 edition shows that the station buildings faced south and were not at the ends of the tracks as at most termini.

2. A photograph from about 1910 shows platforms 5 and 6 to be still devoid of a canopy. They became numbers 1 and 2 on 30th September 1931, when the numbering was reversed. The locomotive is SDJR no. 15, a rebuilt Johnson 4–4–0. (S.C. Nash collection)

3. A 1913 view shows the two longest platforms in the centre. They were then numbered 2 and 3. The end elevation of the goods shed is just visible above the coaches standing at platform 1. The linking of the canopies was an unusual feature. (D. Cullum collection)

4. One of the SDJR 0–4–4 tank locomotives, no. 31, takes water in about 1929. It is standing at the end of the shortest platform, then no. 6, having worked down from Templecombe with a two-coach push-pull set.
(S.C. Nash collection)

6. In addition to the S&D route, Bournemouth West handled trains from the Weymouth, Swanage, Brighton, West Moors and Waterloo lines. An ex-LSWR class N15 hauls its train from Waterloo under the impressive down home signal gantry. The line in the foreground once had an inspection pit at the outer end of the platform.
(Lens of Sutton)

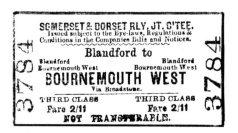

5. A later view of the shunt signals (marked S) shows the spectacles to have been partially masked to reduce the risk of confusion with the starting signals. No. 47 is an ex-LSWR class M7 and is seen with another push-pull set working the Ringwood via Christchurch service. (Lens of Sutton)

7. This April 1947 photograph shows LMS 4–6–0 class 5 no. 4844 at the head of a train for Bath while SR 4–4–0 class L12 no. 429 stands at platform 2. The canopy here was an SR sheet steel construction and contrasted badly with the other two. (S. W. Baker)

→

9. The spans between the canopies would have reduced the risk of them blowing away in a gale, as happened at Bognor. On the right are the signs for the station master's office and the refreshment room which was on platform 4. (Lens of Sutton)

0030
Somerset & Dorset Rly.
Joint Committee.
Issued subject to the Bye-laws
Regulations & Conditions in the
Companies Bills and Notices.
OFFICER ON LEAVE.
Bournemouth West to
SHILLINGSTONE
Via Broadstone
First Class
NOT TRANSFERABLE.
‑ ‑ ‑ ‑ ‑ ‑ ‑ ‑ ‑ ‑ ‑ ‑ ‑ ‑ ‑
Somerset & Dorset Rly.
Joint Committee.
OFFICER ON LEAVE.
Shillingstone
Bournem'th W.
Shillingstone to
BOURNEM'TH WEST
Via Broadstone
First Class
0030

5252 Somerset & Dorset Rly. Jt. C'tee.
Issued subject to the Bye-laws, Regulations &
Conditions in the Companies Bills & Notices.
Sturminster Newton to
Sturminster Newton   Sturminster Newton
Bournemouth West   Bournemouth West
BOURNEMOUTH WEST **5252**
Via Broadstone
THIRD CLASS   THIRD CLASS
Fare 4/3   Fare 4/3
NOT TRANSFERABLE.

8051 SOUTHERN RAILWAY.
Issued subject to the Bye-laws, Regulations &
Conditions in the Company's Bills and Notices.
Bournemouth West to
Bournemouth West   Bournemouth West
Bournemouth Cen.   Bournemouth Cen.
BOURNEMOUTH CEN. **8051**
FIRST CLASS   FIRST CLASS
Fare 9½d.   Fare 9½d.
NOT TRANSFERABLE.

8. No. 53807 was one of a small batch of 2–8–0s built specially to work heavy freight trains over the steeply graded northern part of the S&D. It was pressed into passenger service on 6th August 1960 and is seen at platform 6, standing on a fouling bar, well clear of the splintered buffer stop. (H.N. James)

10. Platform 4 was the longest and yet barely accommodates the "Bournemouth Belle". Devoid of the once famous head-

board, Merchant Navy class no. 35017 *Belgian Marine* blows off prior to leaving for Waterloo, on 6th June 1966. (S.C. Nash)

11. Over ½ mile north of the station, the 1888 route to Bournemouth East diverged eastwards on a sharp curve, seen in front of Bournemouth West Junction box on 18th September 1926. In the background is Branksome locomotive shed, built inside the triangular junction in about 1890 to house the engines for the SDJR services. (Late E. Wallis)

12. The 9.03am from Bristol speeds towards its destination on 7th July 1962, headed by ex-LMS class 5 no. 44804, while an up local train passes Bournemouth West Junction box. The 20 mph restriction applies to the curve to Bournemouth Central which was abandoned in November 1965.
(A.G. Thorpe)

13. Passenger services to Bournemouth West ceased on 4th October 1965 but trains from the S&D route were diverted to Bournemouth Central from 2nd August of that year. The terminus was eventually demolished and the land was used for part of Wessex Way. In 1966–67, the remaining area was used for erection of a carriage shed, inspection shed and numerous sidings for electric stock. The former Bournemouth West Junction box was retained to control entry to the sidings and is seen here in 1982. (J. Scrace)

BRANKSOME

The 1924 map shows the S&D locomotive shed and turntable at the Bournemouth West end of the triangular junction, the lines at the top of the right hand page being those to Bournemouth Central. At the top of the left hand page is a branch to the Sharp Jones Pottery. The sidings in the centre of the triangle were for domestic coal and general goods, and were lifted in 1970. The curve on the right ceased to be used after 1st November 1965 and was lifted in 1968.

14. A view west in August 1927 shows the two-road S&D locomotive shed, the turntable being located by the locomotive on the right. In its final years, five sets of loco crews were rostered here but only one pair of men worked through to Bath each day.
(R. Shepherd)

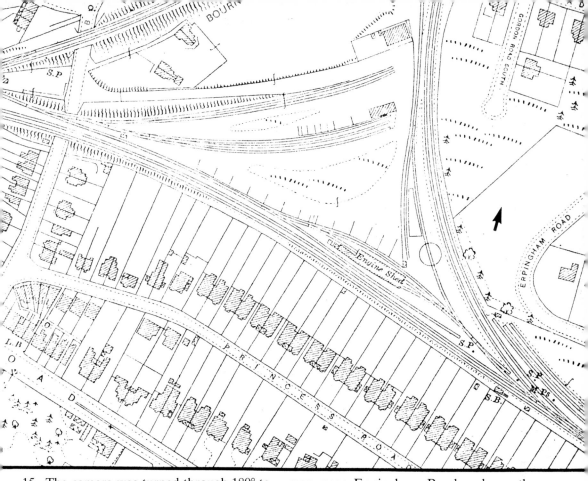

15. The camera was turned through 180° to show a light engine returning tender first from Bournemouth West. The carriages on the left are standing in sidings, marked on the map near Eppingham Road and, on the right, the roof of the West Junction box just shows above the clerestories. (R. Shepherd)

16. Another of the former S&DJR's heavy freight 7Fs is seen after a summer flight south from its northern habitat, on 5th August 1950. Although apparently about to run onto the turntable, this class was too long to use it and had to turn on the triangle. Built for the SDJR in 1925 as no. 89, this locomotive is now preserved at the Midland Railway Centre. (C.L. Caddy collection)

17. Now an exhibit at the Manchester Liverpool Road Station Museum, ex-LMS class 5 no. 44806 runs towards the terminus on 24th May 1961, with its rake of ex SR coaches. The shed was closed on 1st January 1963 and demolished in 1965, the crews being transferred to Bournemouth Central depot. (A.G. Thorpe)

18. The cottage at the west end of the triangle remained standing in 1987, the year in which an ex-S&DJR class 7F was returned to full working order on the West Somerset Railway. It was no. 88 (BR no. 53808), sister to no. 53806, seen approaching Branksome down platform on 9th September 1961 with the 11.12am to Sheffield. (A.G. Thorpe)

19. The station was opened on 1st June 1893, nearly 20 years after the line. An island platform had been planned, similar to the first station at Pokesdown, shown in picture no. 101 in our *Southampton to Bournemouth* album. The canopies have been cut back in stages and were finally removed in August 1987. (Lens of Sutton)

20. A view from the up platform on 2nd July 1963 shows a typical S&D line local train, hauled by BR class 2 no. 41243. The 20 mph restriction sign applied to trains for Bournemouth West. (A.G. Thorpe)

21. The transition scene in 1969 shows only one of the four semaphore signal arms remaining and that approach to the carriage siding was controlled by two ground signals. The conductor rail was extended west to this station, where all electric stock has to reverse to and from the depot. (J. Scrace)

PARKSTONE

22. This was the only intermediate station when the Broadstone–Poole branch was extended to Bournemouth (West) on 15th June 1874. An early postcard shows an up train under the fully glazed footbridge. (Lens of Sutton)

The 1924 map shows a branch running south from the goods yard. It was about 1¼ miles long and ran to Wragg & Son's South Western Pottery and Salterns Pier.

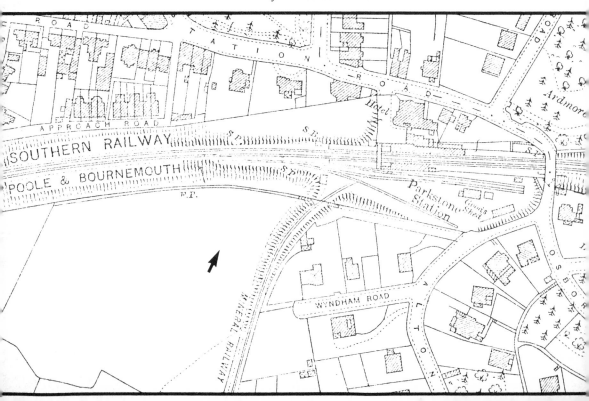

23. 4–4–0s were first used on S&D services in 1891. No. 45 is seen here in 1925, displaying its deeply waisted chimney and its unusu-ally forward dome. The signal box was on the up side and closed in 1933. (D. Cullum collection)

24. Two class 4Fs pass through Parkstone with a train from the S&D route on 5th August 1950 – another case of goods engines being pressed into passenger service in the summer. The line of washing could have come in grey on a busy Saturday. No. 44100 was ex-LMS and no. 43875 was built by the Midland Railway. (S.W. Baker)

25. The sign proclaims "Parkstone for Sandbanks", a residential area 2½ miles to the south, from where a ferry across the mouth of Poole Harbour links with a direct road to Swanage. Ex-SR Q class 0–6–0 no. 30539 fails to totally obscure the coal staithes and goods shed. (Lens of Sutton)

26. A 1963 view towards Bournemouth shows that the footbridge has lost its roof but that the platforms retained their gas lights. The gradient post shows 1 in 50 down to Parkstone Bay – in fact the incline is mostly at 1 in 60, still a stiff climb for locomotives with long trains loaded with holidaymakers from the North. (C.L. Caddy)

POOLE

27. This is the town's first station and was the terminus of the branch from Broadstone from 2nd December 1872 until 15th June 1874. This 1875 view from the High Street footbridge shows the station to lack a similar bridge and that only a single track was laid initially. It was doubled in 1885 and from 1888 it was possible to travel to London via the direct route through Bournemouth. (Poole Museum)

28. A postcard gives a closer look at the old station, with its mixture of canopies and awkward sharply curved platforms. The lattice footbridge survived until the station was rebuilt. (Lens of Sutton)

29. The 2.00pm Templecombe to Bournemouth West slows down for the compulsory stop at Poole on 23rd February 1938. The locomotive is LMS class 4F no. 4557. The unusual gas lamp brackets span the line to Poole Quay, a once important commercial venue. The size of the goods shed also reflects the importance of Poole as a trading centre. (D.H. Wakely/J.R.W. Kirkby collection)

The 1925 survey has the line from Bournemouth on the right, together with one of the sidings of the once extensive Poole Gasworks. Below the station, a siding is seen to run into the street. It continued along West Quay Road, for nearly ¾ mile, to the quay east of Poole Bridge and was in use until 1960. Above the station the street tramway is shown. This was part of the Bournemouth passenger tramways which were in use from 1901 to 1936.

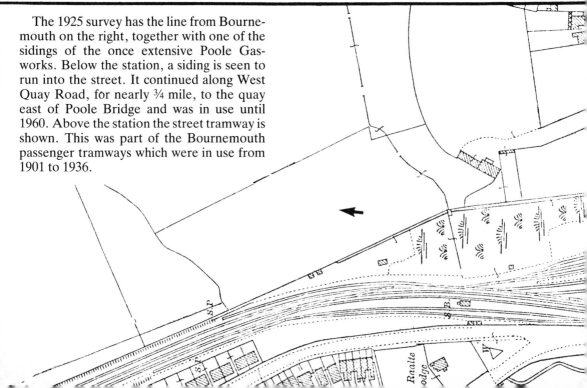

30. A camera on the station footbridge in 1959 records the Towngate Street level crossing, which was replaced by a concrete bridge in 1971. In the background is the High Street footbridge, partly obscured by the exhaust of one of the class 2P 4–4–0s, used for many years on S&D passenger services. (F.W. Ivey)

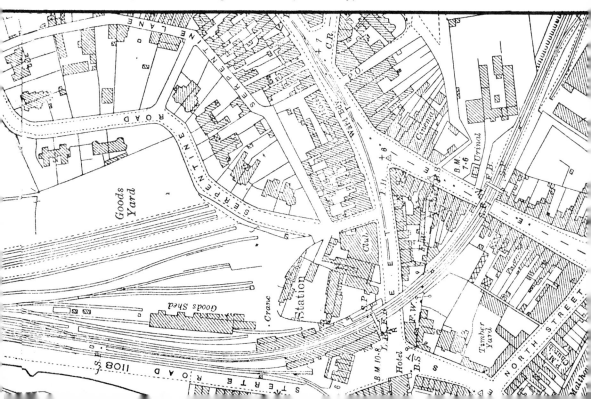

31. All passenger trains are obliged to stop at Poole, even the "Pines Express", although it mainly conveyed the crowds to Bournemouth. "West Country" class no. 34043 *Combe Martin* appears to carry the well-known gloves and beret of Peter Smith. (C.L. Caddy)

32. A 1966 photograph from the High Street footbridge shows Poole 'A' Box, 'B' Box being to the west of the station and still in use in 1987. Almost everything in this view has been lost in recent years. The crossing is now only used by pedestrians and the gates were replaced by lifting barriers in November 1977, cotrolled by 'B' Box under CCTV. (D. Cullum)

HOLES BAY JUNCTION

33. ¾-mile north of Poole station the lines divided, the 1872 route to Broadstone being on the right and the 1893 line to Hamworthy Junction on the left. This is the only photograph we have seen that includes the signal box, which was closed on 28th October 1934. (Late E. Wallis)

34. A 1966 photograph from the same bridge makes it clear that the line west was built on an embankment, which ran across the middle of Holes Bay. The diverging points were worked by power from Poole West (later 'B') Box, the trailing points being unworked. Military sidings were laid down at the end of WWI, on the site of the buildings on the right. (D. Cullum)

CREEKMOOR HALT

35. Sounding like a cure for arthritis, this halt was built almost entirely of pre-cast concrete components and was opened on 19th June 1933. It was the last stopping place to come into use on the route and remained open to the end of passenger services. A lone passenger awaits the arrival of a Bath – Bournemouth service on 8th August 1962, hauled by the BR class 4MT now to be found on the Bluebell Railway. (R.M. Casserley)

36. A footbridge and level crossing were located at the north end of the halt. Further south, a siding was provided (until 1969) for Sykes Pottery, the buildings of which are in the background. On the other side of the track, a siding ran into a Ministry of Supply depot from 1940 until 1959. (D. Cullum)

37. The level crossing was over a minor road and the gates were worked by hand. The track on the left was retained until 1977, as far as Wimbrone, but the other one was abandoned in 1970. Both photographs were taken on 31st March 1966. (D. Cullum)

BROADSTONE

38. This faded postcard reveals that even the final station buildings were insignificant, particularly when compared with the Railway Hotel, on the right, and the covered footbridge to the four lengthy platforms. (Lens of Sutton)

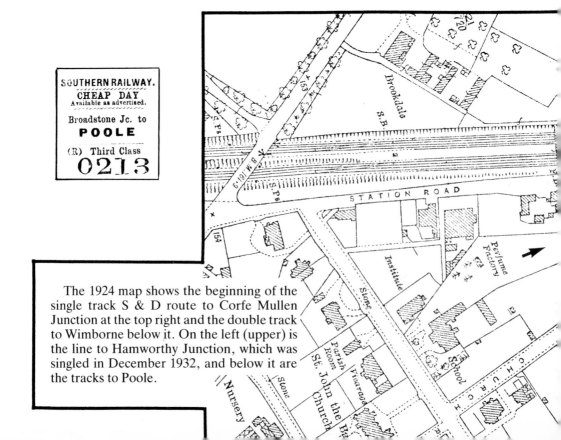

SOUTHERN RAILWAY.
CHEAP DAY
Available as advertised.
Broadstone Jc. to
POOLE
(R) Third Class
0213

The 1924 map shows the beginning of the single track S & D route to Corfe Mullen Junction at the top right and the double track to Wimborne below it. On the left (upper) is the line to Hamworthy Junction, which was singled in December 1932, and below it are the tracks to Poole.

39. The rear coaches are still on the single track of the S & D line while no. 34043 *Combe Martin* runs onto the branch to Holes Bay Junction, the platforms for which were added in 1874. Part of the goods yard is seen in this 1959 photograph. It closed in October 1965. (A.G. Thorpe)

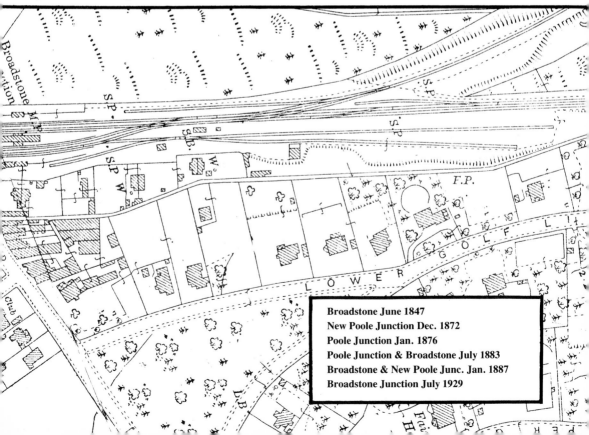

Broadstone June 1847
New Poole Junction Dec. 1872
Poole Junction Jan. 1876
Poole Junction & Broadstone July 1883
Broadstone & New Poole Junc. Jan. 1887
Broadstone Junction July 1929

40. To minimise delays on the single line sections, automatic tablet catchers were designed and installed by Alfred Whitaker. The hoop of the small pouch containing the tablet is seen above the centre driving wheel. The projecting part of the lineside post retracted as soon as the transfer had taken place. (E. Wilmshurst)

42. No. 75027 is seen again, piloting "West Country" class no. 34045 *Ottery St. Mary* at the head of a train from Nottingham, on 24th June 1961. The reverse curves of platforms 1 and 2 are evident in this view. Now, the entire site is covered by houses. (A.G. Thorpe)

41. This is the 7.45 am Bradford to Bournemouth West hauled by BR class 9F no. 92001, on 1st September 1962. The Hamworthy Junction line on the left lost its passenger service in May 1964 and closed altogether in June 1966. The ground frame and crossover remained usable until July 1969. (S.C. Nash)

43. In 1970, the track through platform 1 to Holes Bay Junction and the remaining part of the S & D was lifted. This picture shows work in progress on 4th April – on 18th October, the signal box was closed and then only a single track remained to Wimborne. (J.H. Bird)

CORFE MULLEN

44. The 1855 single line cut-off, which avoided reversal at Wimborne, was steeply graded and reached a summit on the golf course. A little to the north, a halt was provided from 5th July 1928 until 17th September 1956, for the residential area of East End. This is the state of affairs in 1965 – no trace remains now as the cutting has been filled in. (C.L. Caddy)

45. 1¼ miles west of the halt, the single line from Broadstone joins the original route from Wimborne, seen here on the right in 1934. The line lost its passenger service on 11th July 1920 but milk trains continued to use the route until 17th June 1933. Thereafter the line was cut back to Carter's clay siding, about a mile distant, and was shunted by down goods trains until 19th September 1959. The water works, in the background, was built in 1915 and provided with a siding for its coal supply. The buildings are now much squatter, the pumps having been converted to electrical power.
(D. Cullum collection)

◄——————

46. The signal box, photographed in 1965, controlled the single line from Broadstone (the tablet catcher is seen on the right), the double track to Bailey Gate (doubled through to Blandford in 1901-02) and the level crossing gates, by means of a wheel.
(C.L. Caddy)

47. The moment of transfer of the tablet was captured on film at 1.18pm on 24th April 1965. The squat Norman tower of St. Hubert's Church is visible above the dome. This continues to survive the passage of time, as do the crossing gates and cottage.
(C.L. Caddy)

BAILEY GATE

The tiny village of Corfe Mullen was situated north of the line, half way between the junction and Bailey Gate Crossing, which was 1½ miles east of the station of that name. Located on the banks of the River Stour, the massive mill is still an obvious feature of the village, which contains an interesting mixture of dwellings of considerable antiquity. The new Corfe Mullen is an extensive area of housing, well to the south of the old village, forming a continuous urban area from Broadstone and Bournemouth.

BAILEY GATE CROSSING

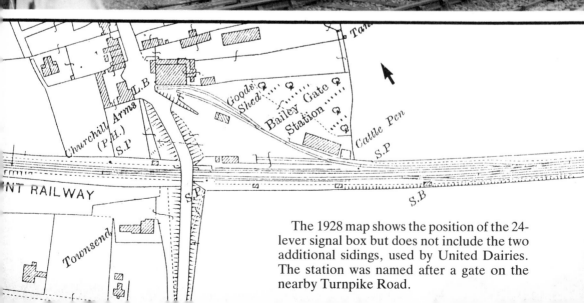

The 1928 map shows the position of the 24-lever signal box but does not include the two additional sidings, used by United Dairies. The station was named after a gate on the nearby Turnpike Road.

48. Only ½ mile from Corfe Mullen Junction, this box was 1½ miles from Bailey Gate and controlled the crossing of the busy A31. The cottage continues to be occupied but little remains of the box, which was on the down side of the line. It ceased to be a block post in 1923 and no longer controlled entry to the two Admiralty sidings on the down side. (C.L. Caddy)

49. Named Sturminster Marshall until the line was extended to include a station at Sturminster Newton, Bailey Gate served a population of about 1200 (in later years), despatched vast tonnages of dairy products and had a substantial seasonal traffic of watercress and mushrooms. (C.L. Caddy)

50. The station was set amidst the well-watered green meadows of the Stour Valley and recognised the nearby village on its nameboard. The rustic seat and the small mountain of empty whey barrels, in this 1965 photograph, reflect its rural setting and main function. (C.L. Caddy)

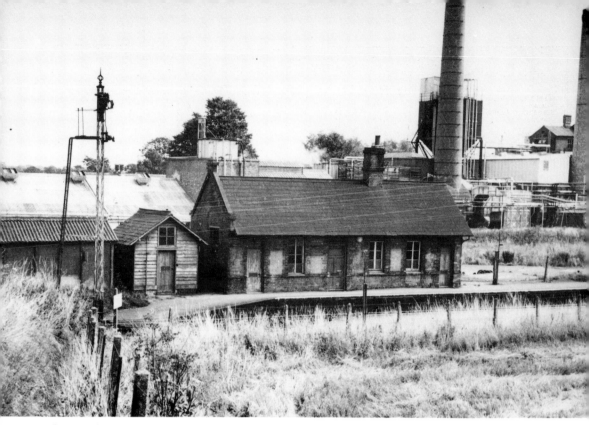

51. A view of the modest passenger facilities, six months later after they were closed, includes part of the massive dairy complex and its two boiler house chimneys. The site now contains a large number of small industrial units, only one of which is used for cheese making by Unigate Dairies. (D. Cullum)

52. Diesel traction was never employed regularly on the S & D route, it being the last outpost of steam on the Western Region in its final months. Class 33 no. 6506 groans south on 4th April 1970, with lifted track materials, while residents and railwaymen alike continued to complain about the closure. The goods yard here had been closed on 5th April 1965. (J.H. Bird)

THROUGH COMMUNICATION,

CARDIFF TO POOLE, (FOR BOURNEMOUTH) LONDON, SOUTHAMPTON, PORTSMOUTH, GOSPORT, ISLE OF WIGHT, LYMINGTON, WEYMOUTH, SALISBURY, YEOVIL, CHARD, HONITON, EXETER, EXMOUTH BARNSTAPLE, BIDEFORD, &c.

[* *Passengers may be booked through from Cardiff to all Stations.*

		Class 1, 2, 3.	Class 1, 2. **A**	Class 1, 2.	Class 1, 2.	Class 1, 2	Class 1, 2.
		a.m.	a.m.	p.m.	p.m.	p.m.	p.m.
*CARDIFF, by Steamer to Burnham		8 0	10 40	12 55	12 55	4 5	6 40
Burnham	depart	8 12	11 0	1 15	1 15	4 20	7 15
HIGHBRIDGE Junction	,,	8 50	11 17	1 40	1 40	4 50	7 45
Glastonbury	arrive	9 55	11 45	2 0	2 0	5 12	8 0
Wells	,,	9 17	11 40			5 38	
Pylle (Shepton Mallet) (Per Bus	,,	9 35	11 51	2 20	2 20	6 6	...
Cole (Bruton & Castle Carey) (Per Bus	,,	9 47	12 1	2 30	2 30	6 22	...
Wincanton	,,	10 0	12 10	2 37	3 37	6 38	...
TEMPLE COMBE Junction	,,						

		via Temple Combe.	via Wimborne.	via Temple Combe.	via Wimborne.	via Temple Combe.	via Wimborne.	via Temple Combe.	via Wimborne.	via Temple Combe.	via Wimborne.	via Temple Combe.	via Wimborne.
Salisbury	,,	11 20	...	1 15	...	...	...	4 14	...	7 44	...	...	
Southampton	,,	...	1 7	3 30	2 53	...	...	5 40	7 9	7 21	12 57	...	
Gosport	,,	1 47	...	3 46	3 46	...	...	5 57	8 15	...	...	...	
Portsmouth	,,	2 0	...	4 0	4 0	...	...	6 10	8 28	10 0	...	...	
LONDON (Waterloo Station) ...	,,	2 15	...	4 20	5 50	...	...	6 47	...	10 40	...	...	
Yeovil	,,	11 0	...	...	...	2 31	...	4 2	...	8 7	...	...	
Chard	,,	12 45	...	...	...	...	...	4 50	...	8 50	...	...	
Honiton	,,	1 12	...	...	...	3 18	...	5 8	...	9 10	...	...	
Exeter	,,	2 0	...	...	...	3 48	...	5 50	...	9 45	...	...	
Exmouth	,,	...	...	...	...	4 23	...	6 40	...	10 20	...	...	
Barnstaple	,,	4 27	...	...	...	5 28	...	8 11	...	...	...	...	
Bideford	,,	4 50	...	...	...	5 50	...	8 38	...	...	...	...	
Weymouth	,,	...	1 15	...	4 0	...	...	...	8 10	...	10 10	...	
Lymington, for Freshwater, Isle of Wight	,,	...	...	...	2 47	...	...	...	7 0	...	...	...	

TEMPLE COMBE Junction (S. W. Station)	depart	10 14	12 24	2 40	2 40	7 40	...
Sturminster Newton	arrive	10 36	12 43	3 0	3 0	8 5	...
Blandford	,,	11 5	1 3	3 25	3 25	8 27	...
WIMBORNE Junction (see Temple Combe)	,,	11 40	1 26	3 45	3 45	8 53	...
POOLE	,,	12 15	2 5	4 5	4 5	9 25	...
BOURNEMOUTH, by Omnibus ... about		1 30	3 15	5 15	5 15	...	...

Swanage, by steamer, from Poole advertised to leave at 10 15 a.m. and 4 p.m on Mondays and Thursdays commencing 15th of May

(Right margin, vertical): A Third class to London from Burnham and Highbridge.

THROUGH COMMUNICATION,

BIDEFORD, BARNSTABLE, EXMOUTH, EXETER, HONITON, CHARD, YEOVIL, SALISBURY, WEYMOUTH, LYMINGTON, ISLE OF WIGHT, GOSPORT, PORTSMOUTH, SOUTHAMPTON, LONDON, AND POOLE, (FROM BOURNEMOUTH AND SWANAGE) TO CARDIFF, AND SOUTH WALES.

		Class 1, 2, 3.	Class 1, 2, 3.	Class 1,2.	Class 1,2.	Class 1, 2.	Class 1, 2.
		...	a.m.	a.m.	a.m.		
Swanage (By Steamer to Poole) ...	,,	Advertised to	ply on Mondays	and Thursdays	commencing 15th May.		
BOURNEMOUTH, by Omnibus	depart.	a.m.		8 45	10 40	1 20	
POOLE	,,		8 10	10 15	1 20	5 25	
WIMBORNE JUNCTION (see Temple Combe)	,,		8 35	10 40	1 50	6 0	
Blandford...	,,		9 5	11 5	2 20	6 32	
Sturminster Newton	,,		9 30	11 34	2 43	6 55	
TEMPLE COMBE JUNCTION	arrive		10 0	12 6	3 12	7 20	

		via Wimborne.	via Temple Combe.	via Wimborne.	via Temple Combe.	via Wimborne.	via Temple Combe.	via Wimborne.	via Temple Combe.	via Wimborne.	via Temple Combe.	via Wimborne.	via Temple Combe.
Lymington, from Freshwater, and Isle of Wight ...	depart	...	...	...	...	...	...	10 20	...	1 40	...	...	...
Weymouth	,,	...	...	6 25	...	8 35	...	12 20	...	4 50	...	...	...
Bideford	,,	...	...	...	...	...	7 15	...	11 15	...	2 30	...	...
Barnstaple	,,	...	...	...	...	...	7 36	...	11 35	...	2 54	...	...
Exmouth	,,	...	...	...	7 30	...	10 0	...	1 25	...	5 5	...	...
Exeter	,,	...	...	...	8 9	...	10 39	...	1 57	...	5 40	...	...
Honiton	,,	...	...	...	8 25	...	11 0	...	12 10	...	5 50	...	...
Chard	,,	...	...	...	9 35	...	11 35	...	2 40	...	6 30	...	...
Yeovil	,,	...	...	...	...	...	7 5	...	11 42	...	3 50	...	...
London (Waterloo Station) ...	,,	...	...	...	...	...	7 55	7 55	10 50	11 40	4 15	...	...
Portsmouth ...	,,	...	...	...	...	10 25	8 50	10 25	11 40	1 24	4 50	...	...
Gosport ...	,,	...	...	6 0	...	10 25	8 50	10 25	11 40	1 24	4 50	...	...
Southampton...	,,	...	...	6 0	...	10 25	8 50	10 25	11 40	1 24	4 50	...	...
Salisbury	,,	...	...	7 20	...	...	10 15	...	1 13	...	6 34	...	...

TEMPLE COMBE Junction (S. W. Station.)	,,	...	10 14	12 24	3 34	7 40	...
Wincanton	,,	...	10 25	12 35	3 50	7 52	...
Cole (Bruton & Castle Carey) (Per Bus	,,	...	10 35	12 45	4 2	8 13	...
Pylle (Shepton Mallett) Per Bus	,,	depart	10 48		4 18	8 27	...
WELLS	arrive	8 0	11 35	2 0	6 5	9 5	...
Glastonbury	,,	8 18	11 20	1 13	4 40	8 47	...
Burnham	,,	9 20	12 8	2 10	5 45	9 30	...
CARDIFF, by Steamer from Burnham,							

SPETISBURY

Spetisbury is an attractive linear village set out along the A350 main road for nearly a mile. Located on a shelf on the chalk hill side, it is situated in the narrow Stour Gap. The engineers took advantage of this feature and had to construct the railway parallel to and slightly above the village which retains a rich variety of buildings, many of which are still thatched.

53. A northward view dated 1895 shows the widening work in progress with one fresh chalk face in the cutting and new material on the embankment. The disc and crossbar signal (used to request trains to stop) survived until the double track came into use in 1901, when a signal box was built near its site. (D. Cullum collection)

54. The station lost its staff in August 1934 and became "Spetisbury Halt". A later look north reveals that the 1901 buildings were more spacious than those on the down platform and that the platform lighting was minimal. (A.W. Burges)

55. The halt was closed on 10th August 1952, this 1965 photograph showing the southward view more familiar to southbound locomotive crews in the later years of the line. Concrete sleepers were uncommon on the S & D and were laid not long before closure. (C.L. Caddy)

56. With the Stour Gap and some of the attractive dwellings of Spetisbury in the background, class 3 no. 77014 runs south on 16th October 1966, over 6 months after the last public passenger train. This LCGB special ran from Waterloo via Haslemere and Fareham, visiting Ringwood and Hamworthy Goods on its return journey. (J. Scrace)

CHARLTON MARSHALL

57. Like Spetisbury, this village is attractively located on the side of the Stour Valley. It was provided with a halt, close to the village centre, on 5th July 1928. It officially closed on 17th September 1956 but continued to be used by pupils of Clayesmore Preparatory School at the beginning and end of each term. The sign still remained in place when photographed on 6th March 1966. (J. Scrace)

58. The route crossed the River Stour ¼ mile south of Blandford Forum station, the lattice span being flanked by two pairs of flood arches. These were almost in use as the river rose, in October 1966, prior to the passage of the LCGB special train, seen earlier at Spetisbury. (J. Scrace)

BLANDFORD FORUM

The town is not of Roman origin despite its latin suffix, which seems to have been added in the 19th century. It has been an important market town for many centuries but in 1731 a disastrous fire destroyed the entire town centre. By 1760, it had been rebuilt to the present pleasing form, being dominated by the parish church, arguably one of the finest Georgian provincial churches. Although the first railway station was a temporary one, a mile south of the town, the presence of a station near the town centre did much to strengthen the town's commercial position in the Victorian era. The railway did not use "Forum" until 1953!

59. A photograph dated 1898 shows the crew of a southbound train exchanging tablets with the signalman. Like the town earlier, his box was destroyed by fire. It was struck by lightning on 23rd June 1906, having been erected in 1893. (D. Cullum collection)

SOMERSET & DORSET J. RY. This Ticket is issued subject to the regulations & Conditions stated on the Time Tables & Bills of the Joint Line.
PARLIAMENTARY. THIRD CLASS.
STALBRIDGE to
BLANDFORD
FARE 1s. 0½d.   FARE 1s. 0½d.
Blandford   Blandford

60. No.23 was one of six 0–6–0s acquired in 1874 to work the extension of the S & D over the Mendips to Bath. They were built by John Fowler & Co. of Leeds, who later became famous for their ploughing engines, some of which are still to be seen each autumn at work at the nearby steam rally. (D. Cullum collection)

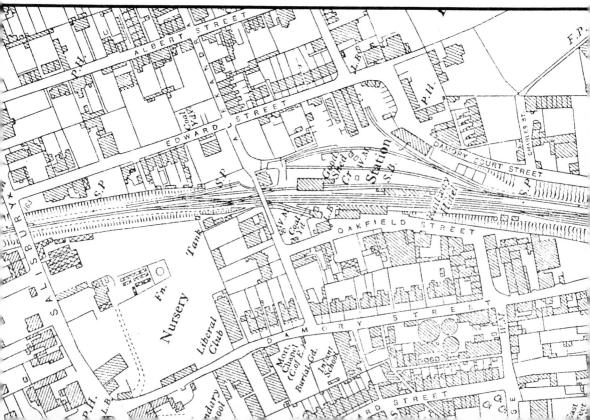

61. A view south from the public footbridge shows two wagons in the tiny coal yard. Coal was also unloaded in the main goods yard. The railway was slow to change to electric lighting, although the town had a 100 volt 20 amp generator as early as 1914. A generating station was eventually built adjacent to the goods yard and a siding was extended into it. (Lens of Sutton)

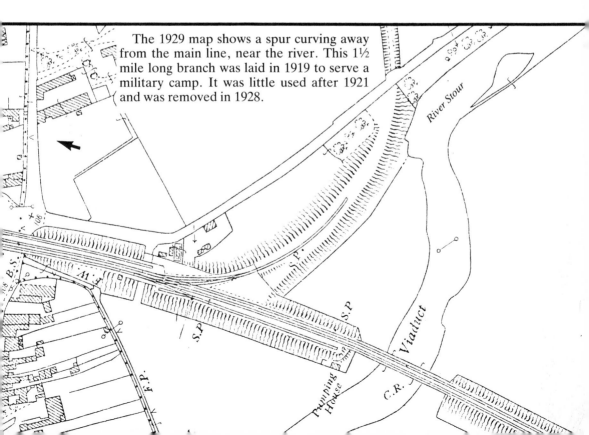

The 1929 map shows a spur curving away from the main line, near the river. This 1½ mile long branch was laid in 1919 to serve a military camp. It was little used after 1921 and was removed in 1928.

62. The Somerset Central Railway had its offices adjacent to Blandford station. The rear of this building is seen on the right of the previous picture – coal for the office fire did not have to be carried far. As at Guildford, a drinking fountain can be seen in the wall – a blessing for passengers and employees alike. (D. Cullum collection)

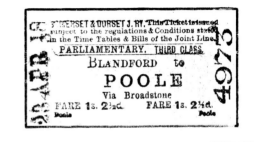

63. One of the popular class 9Fs is coupled to an ex-LNER coach marshalled at the front of a train from Manchester on 7th July 1962, the last year of through working. Part of a siding remains today, set into the road near the former goods yard gates (above the word "Station" on the map). To add to the pathos, a spoked wagon wheel has been welded to it! (C.L. Caddy)

64. After the Western Region took control of the line, some ex-GWR 57xx class Pannier tanks were sent to work the local freight services. No. 4631 is seen on 7th August 1964, shunting the busy yard which remained open long after the last passenger had left, closing on 6th January 1969. (J.H. Bird)

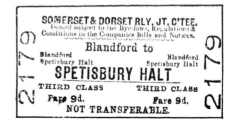

65. A short while later, the same engine moves its train of fertiliser vans onto the single line before setting them back into the down platform. Included in this view are the end-loading dock, the goods shed, the signal box and the lofty up starting signal. The footbridge was for the general public, a subway being provided for passengers. A footpath now passes under the bridge and a set of buffer stops stands as the only other railway remnant in the town. (J.H. Bird)

66. The hoop of a large tablet pouch projects from the cab as LMS designed class 2MT no. 41283 passes the goods shed and water column on 13th August 1965. The sign mentions Bryanston School, which generated traffic at term ends, but the Grammar School produced a regular railway revenue from its day pupils. (J.H. Bird)

BLANDFORD.

SHUNTERS' BELL SIGNALS from NORTH END of the YARD to the SIGNAL-BOX.

Reverse Goods Shed Points	1	beat of the Bell.
Up Train Ready	2	beats ,, ,,
Reverse Loop Points	3	,, ,, ,,
Set Points for Up Main Line and Langton Siding ...	4	,, ,, ,,
Set Points for Up Main Line and East Street Siding	5	,, ,, ,,
Reverse Points for Horse Box Siding	7	,, ,, ,,
Reverse Points for Snow's Coal Siding	8	,, ,, ,,

SHUNTERS' BELL SIGNALS from the SOUTH END of the YARD to the SIGNAL-BOX.

Reverse Yard Points	1	beat of the Bell.
Reverse Cross-over Points	2	beats ,, ,,
Reverse Langton Siding Points	3	,, ,, ,,
Reverse East Street Siding Points from Up Siding to Up Main Line	4	,, ,, ,,
Down Goods Train ready...	5	,, ,, ,,

MIDLAND or other PASSENGER VEHICLES fitted with CLERESTORY ROOFS.

Vehicles of this class must not be shunted into the Sidings underneath the overbridge at Blandford.

67. Evident here, on 24th April 1965, are the 7-ton crane and the cantilevered signal box which projected over the down siding. This was, in fact, a loop passing right through the goods shed, but locomotives were not

allowed to run through the shed. During WWII a canteen was provided on the up platform for the benefit of the large number of troops entrained here. (C.L. Caddy)

STOURPAINE &
DURWESTON HALT

68. A 1958 picture shows an unremunerative southbound freight service and a deserted halt. Not surprising, as it had been closed on 18th December 1951, having opened on 9th July 1928 amid much local jubilation. Half a mile to the north, a passing loop was laid on the down side in 1905. After 1914, the signal box was only manned in the summer and, from 1925 onwards, it was only used on summer Saturdays, or as necessary. (D. Fereday Glenn)

— CLOSING AND OPENING AN INTERMEDIATE SIGNAL BOX ON A SINGLE LINE —

STOURPAINE

8; - INTERLOCKING LEVER

STOURPAINE

To set road for long section working, the following levers must be pulled over;— 8 Half-way, 4, 6, 7, 3, 2, 1, 12, 15 and 8-second half.

To close

Ask Blandford and Shillingstone if they are ready to close section. If so, turn short key for closing. Phone Blandford and Shillingstone and ask them to plunge. When indicator shews 'Lock Off', turn key as far as possible, withdraw it, and take it to lever frame, inserting it in lock on Interlocking Lever, (No. 8), and turning it. Pull No. 8 to middle position, then pull over point and signal levers for through working. Pull Interlocking Lever No. 8 right over, and withdraw long key. Put key in 'Long Section' and turn as far as possible. Phone to Blandford and Shillingstone that closure is effected, and tell them to turn their switches to 'Long Section'.

To open

Ask Blandford and Shillingstone if they are ready to open section. If so, turn long key for opening. Phone Blandford and Shillingstone, and ask them to plunge. When Indicator shews 'Lock Off' turn switch as far as possible and withdraw key. Take key to lever frame and insert it in lock on Interlocking Lever No. 8, and turn it. Push No. 8 to the middle position, then return all points and signals to normal. Return Interlocking Lever No. 8 to normal, and withdraw short key. Put key in 'Short Section', and turn as far as possible. Phone to Blandford and Shillingstone that opening is effected, and tell them to turn their switches to 'Short Section'. Exchange signals with Blandford and Shillingstone on Tyer's Tablet Instruments.

69. The proximity of the halt to Stourpaine is shown by the church. Durweston was also within ½ mile and it is at the school there that the name board from the halt is now preserved, the shelter still awaiting a new use.

70. On 8th March 1964, the Southern Counties Touring Society special was hauled by class 9F no. 92209. Originating from Waterloo, the route was via Hounslow, Ascot,

Each autumn, the rolling chalk downs resound to the echoes of the whistles of steam engines – alas not rail mounted – as the gigantic annual steam rally takes place. (C.L. Caddy)

Reading, Basingstoke, Templecombe, Blandford, Hamworthy Junction, Bournemouth and Winchester. (S.C. Nash)

SHILLINGSTONE

Situated at the northern end of the Stour Gap, the chalk hills of Cranborne Chase rise to 600-700ft each side of the railway route, which continues to run roughly parallel to the river and main road. The station was at the northern end of the mile long village (population then 724) which lines the A357 road. Its alternative name is Shilling Okeford; Child Okeford and Okeford Fitzpaine are attractive and substantial downfoot villages on opposite sides of the valley. They once provided considerable agricultural traffic and some passengers at the station.

71. The driver of a northbound train leans out to exchange tablets in about 1898, when the platform edge was still built of timber. Oil lamps and enamelled advertisements complete the vintage scene. (D. Cullum collection)

73. The station staff stands to attention, with mop in hand, as BR class 4 2–6–4T no. 80043 passes through with a Templecombe to Poole stone train on 30th October 1965. Behind the station sign, the bridge carrying the Child Okeford road over the River Stour is visible. (E. Wilmshurst) ⟶

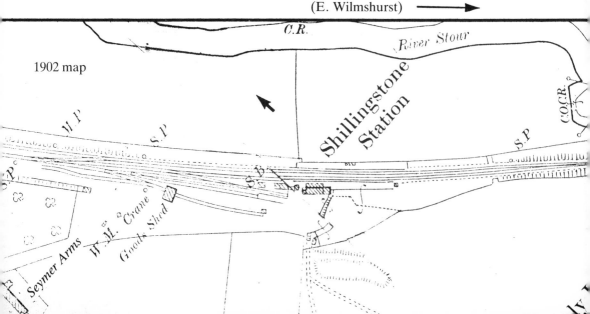

1902 map

72. A northward view in 1962 shows the reconstructed platforms and the station master's greenhouse. Unknown to the railway management, local produce (grown on their premises) was often conveyed by private arrangement with the train crew. (C.L. Caddy)

74. The canopy was the only one between Blandford and Templecombe and was still standing in 1987, on the only station to survive north of Poole. Behind the 16 lever signal box was a small loading dock. (C.L. Caddy)

➡

75. A siding ran through the small goods shed in which this crane was situated. A 5-ton capacity crane was provided in the goods yard which was closed on 5th April 1965. (C. Hall)

STURMINSTER NEWTON

This old market town, with a population of around 1200, stands on a ridge of high land, being surrounded on three sides by the River Stour. Located at the southern extremity of Blackmoor Vale, the quaint Market Place with its randomly set buildings is missed by main road tourists of today and rail travellers of yesterday. The past has been recreated by the restoration to working order of a fine flour mill but evidence of the railway's presence has been totally eliminated, even to the extent of filling the cutting that once passed close to the town.

76. In common with most S & D stations, the up line ran straight through the station, down trains having to reduce speed for the loop. The station was able to benefit from gas lighting, as the gas works was adjacent to the station approach. The line drops at 1 in 80 southwards, in the distance. (Lens of Sutton)

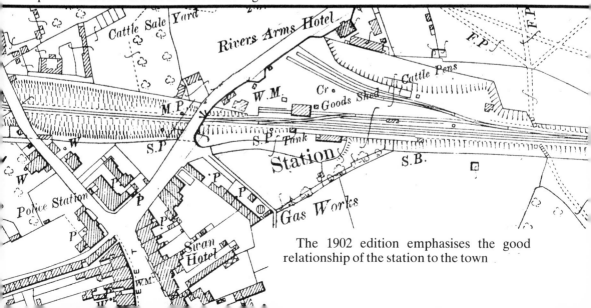

The 1902 edition emphasises the good relationship of the station to the town

77. A northward view in 1962 includes the tablet catcher, the regulation fire buckets, the locomotive water tank and the end of the goods shed, which contained a 30cwt crane.

The up platform retained a primitive feature of early stations – the dropped edge at the foot crossing, seen in close up in the previous photograph. (C.L. Caddy)

STALBRIDGE

A long established town of some 1500 inhabitants, Stalbridge (pronounced Stallbridge) retains some interesting old buildings in the narrow streets, near its centre which was less than ½ mile from the station. As at Shillingstone, it retains its market cross, although here it is a more substantial one, about 30ft high. It has a pleasant location on the gently sloping side of the Stour Valley.

78. The 7-ton crane in the three-siding goods yard is visible in this 1962 northward view. No trace of railway property remains today, except one pair of rails remain visible, obstinately buried in the road at the site of the level crossing. (C.L. Caddy)

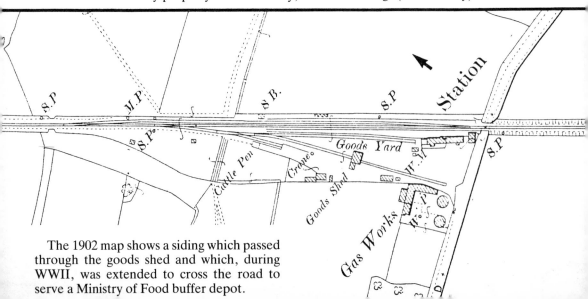

The 1902 map shows a siding which passed through the goods shed and which, during WWII, was extended to cross the road to serve a Ministry of Food buffer depot.

79. Goods traffic ceased in April 1965 and the points were disconnected in July. The signal box had 18 levers and, as it controlled the gates, it remained in use to the end. An ex-Midland Railway 0–6–0 is seen shunting the yard on 17th February 1962. (E. Wilmshurst)

80. Merchant Navy class no. 35011 *General Steam Navigation* speeds towards Stalbridge with the LCGB railtour on 1st January 1966. This was planned to be the last train over the route but hasty postponement of the closure made the tour an anticlimax! (S.C. Nash)

HENSTRIDGE

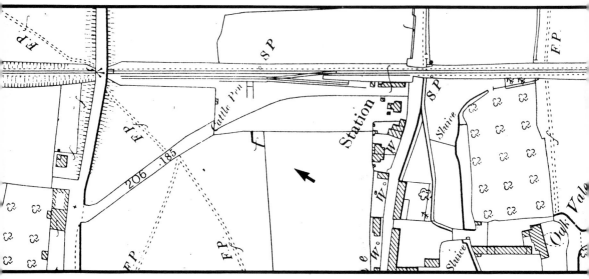

The road crossing the line at the left of this
1903 map is now the A30. There was access to
the station from it, but Blackmoor Lane gave
more direct access from the village.

81. This is the first Somerset station on the
route and also the smallest. It had no passing
loop, no signal box and only one siding, controlled by a ground frame. The points are
visible on the right. The orientation of the
oval disc on the wall indicated to the travel-
ling lineman whether he was required to call
to service the signal or telegraph equipment.
(C.L. Caddy)

82. The term "Station Agent" was used on the S & D – the office holder's house is visible on the right. The 9.40 am from Bournemouth West, all stations to Templecombe, is seen arriving on 5th September 1964. (C.L. Caddy)

83. Although the village was close to hand and it had a population of around 1100, passenger traffic was light. The one-ton crane on the right was located on the corner of the end-loading milk dock. (Lens of Sutton)

TEMPLECOMBE LOWER

The once vast area of railway property at Temple-combe will be considered in four sections – Lower, Shed, Junction and Upper – the order in which a passenger on an up train would see them.

84. A driver approaching from the south could be presented with this view – Temple-combe Up Outer Home on and the short lower platform visible through the arch carrying the main London - Exeter line. Bound for Waterloo on 31st August 1964 is Merchant Navy class no. 35008 *Orient Line*. (J. Scrace)

85. The lower platform would not accommo-date more than two coaches and was a con-siderable walk from the main station. The gate remains in the wall, the path now lead-ing to a private sunken garden. Opened in January 1887, only one light but no name-board was provided, as is evident as class 2MT 2–6–2T no. 41248 accelerates south in March 1959. (D. Fereday Glenn)

86. A 1962 photograph shows the platform's cramped location between Combe Throop Lane bridge and the main line bridge in the background. It was little used by passengers – a rare example in latter years was the last train from Bournemouth on Saturdays, which terminated there at 11.17 pm. The 2.50 am from Bath called regularly, for many years, with mailbags. (C.L. Caddy)

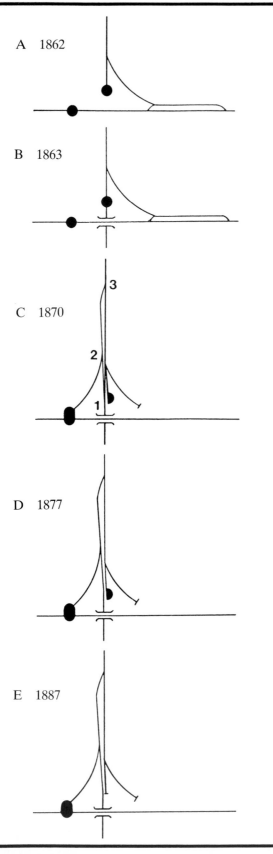

A. The 1860 Gillingham to Sherborne route is shown across the diagram. Somerset Central Railway trains commenced running to a low level terminus in 1862, the connecting spur having been used by construction trains since 1861.

B. The union of the SCR and DCR having taken place (legally in 1862 and physically at Cole), the north-south route was completed but many through trains were routed via the LSWR, involving reversal along their main line. This practice caused traffic congestion, particularly as the LSWR also ran a shuttle service between the stations.

C. A compromise solution was to construct a spur to a platform on the north side of the LSWR station. Three junctions resulted – their numbers are shown. One of the two low level platforms were demolished.

D. In 1877, No.1 junction and its signal box was abolished but some trains from the north contiued to terminate at the former DCR station.

E. The final arrangement came into use in 1887, when the terminus was closed and was replaced by the small lower platform, already illustrated.

87. A view north from Combe Throop Lane on 31st August 1964 shows the S & D water tank adjacent to the spur to the main line station and the gable ends of the original Dorset Central station and house. The former cattle dock is seen in the right foreground as BR class 2 no. 41214 leaves with the 12.23 for Bournemouth West. Until 1887, No. 1 Junction Box was located in the lower left of this view. (J. Scrace)

88. One of the eleven ex-S&DJR 7F 2–8–0s rises up towards the junction on 15th August 1953, with a Bournemouth to Huddersfield relief train. Above it, ex-LMS class 2P 4–4–0 no. 40696 waits at the signal, before completing the operation of pulling the 9.18 am Birmingham to Bournemouth back to the junction. It will then uncouple, allowing the locomotive attached to the other end of the train to take it on south. (S.C. Nash)

89. The first locomotive depot had a single road shed and a 30ft turntable. In 1877, a double road shed was erected and a 50ft turntable soon followed, the white walls of its pit being visible in this 1964 photograph. The DCR stations at Cole and Wincanton were similar to the one seen here, but this one had an upper storey added later. The Junction Box can be seen in the background. (J. Scrace)

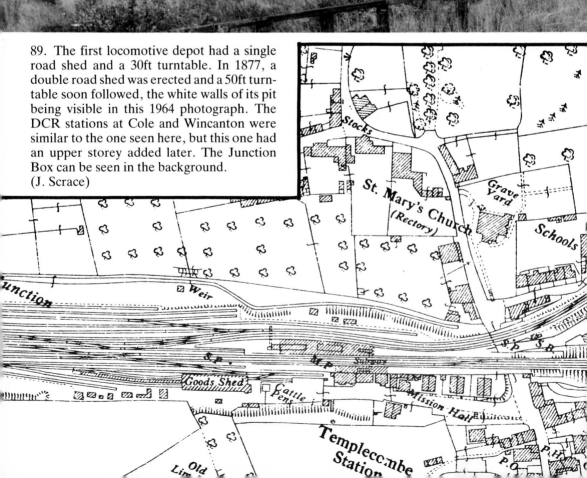

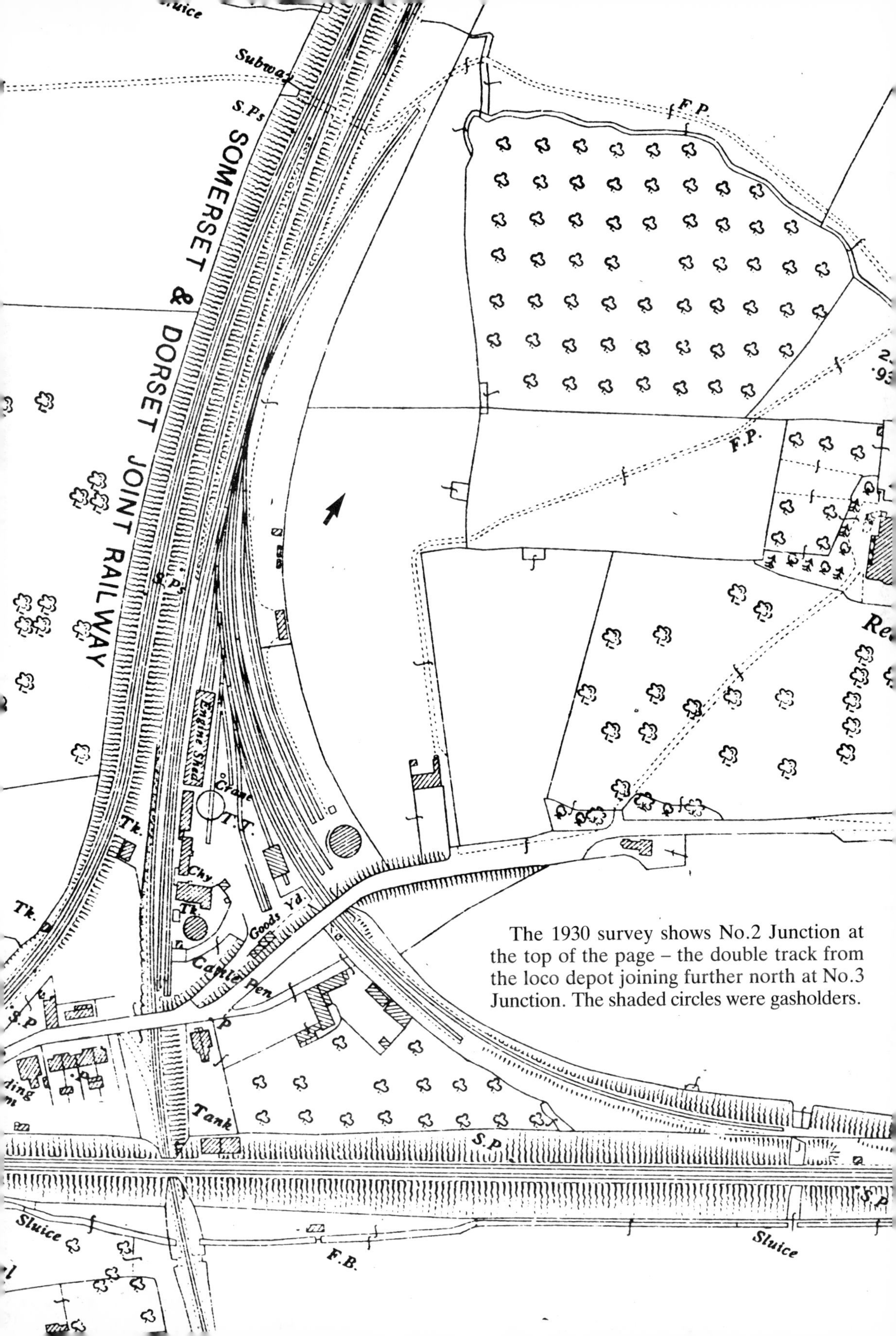

Subway

S.Ps

SOMERSET & DORSET JOINT RAILWAY

F.P.

F.P.

2.
.95

S.Ps

Re.

Engine Shed

Crane
T.T.

Chy

Tk

Goods Yd.

Tk.

Tk.

Tk.

S.P

Cattle Pen

ing
m

Tank

The 1930 survey shows No.2 Junction at
the top of the page – the double track from
the loco depot joining further north at No.3
Junction. The shaded circles were gasholders.

S.P

S.P

Sluice

Sluice

F.B.

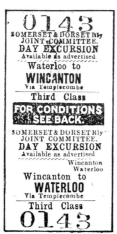

90. The brick-built locomotive shed dated from 1950-51 and now forms part of the premises of Plessey Naval Systems. In June 1965, withdrawn locomotives stood on the curved siding that, until 1870, formed the spur line to the LSWR. The ex-LSWR water tank is evident on the skyline. The lower goods yard remained in use here until 5th May 1950. (S.C. Nash)

⟶

91. An earlier view, from the road bridge on the left of the previous picture, shows that the curved siding extended almost to the Waterloo - Exeter main line, visible in the background. (D. Cullum collection)

92. The "Pines Express" runs onto the single line to Henstridge on 23rd July 1937, its rear coaches still passing the Junction Box. Nos. 631 and 635 will have propelled their train out of the station to the junction, with another locomotive at the other end. (H.C. Casserley)

The origin of the name Templecombe appears to date from 1185 when the Knights *Templar* acquired land in the area. With the expansion of their estates in the West Country, Templecombe became an important administrative cross-roads up to the 14th century. It served as a railway cross roads for a much briefer period. Now, the true cross roads (A30 with the A357) are two miles to the south, near Henstridge, and Templecombe is little more than a village. It has a substantial church which contains a painting thought to have belonged to the Knights Templar and which is remarkably similar to the figure on the Turin Holy Shroud.

93. A view north on 17th February 1962 shows the automatic tablet apparatus, the breakdown crane, and the unusual arrangement of starting signals. The train signalled is the 1.35 pm Templecombe to Bailey Gate, seen restarting after reversing from the station. (E. Wilmshurst)

95. A stopping train for Bournemouth West backs down the double line spur on 11th September 1964, with an ex-GWR Collett 0–6–0 acting as pilot at the far end. The Junction Box is seen in the distance – it was known as "No.2 Junction" to the end, although the other boxes had long gone. (S.W. Baker)

94. The last up "Pines Express" behind *Evening Star*, the last steam locomotive built by BR, passes the site of the No.3 Junction Box. It was on the right and in use until 12th February 1933, when the points were motorised and operated from No.2 Box. At the same time the northern part of the double track from the lower yard was singled, as seen on the left. This simplified the junction. (E. Wilmshurst)

TEMPLECOMBE UPPER

96. An undated photograph of the fine LSWR signal box shows part of its unusual gangway from which it appears that the signalman could observe operations and give flag signals. The locomotive is no. 33 which was designed by Mr. Johnson of the Midland Railway for the S&DJR freight services, although seen here with a rake of 6-wheeled coaches. (Lens of Sutton)

98. The SR almost entirely rebuilt the station in 1938, replacing the subway with a concrete footbridge. Their standard architectural features are visible in this August 1954 view of ex-MR no. 58073 (LMS no. 1382) piloting ex-S&DJR no. 43204. Beyond the coaches of the train from Highbridge, the main line water tank is seen in end view. (H.C. Casserley)

◀━━━

97. A different angle on the same occasion shows the remainder of the gangway, cantilevered out over the up main line. The main station buildings are behind it and a milk van stands in the short up bay. The lack of screw coupling would have given the passengers a rough ride. (Lens of Sutton)

99. The SR provided a new signal box containing 60 levers but BR decided illogically that the entire station should be closed when the S & D route was shut in 1966. Soon only the signal box remained standing but on 3rd October 1983, after considerable local agitation and effort, the station was reopened. As the box by then only contained 16 levers, half the upper floor was adapted as a waiting room and the signalman doubles as booking clerk. Three cheers for all concerned.
(Lens of Sutton)

100. The SR built only eight Z class 0–8–0Ts – one was often to be found at Templecombe, shunting in the upper yard – others performed banking duties from Exeter St. Davids to Central. The track on the right was commonly used by up freight trains leaving the extensive Upper Yard. No. 30953 waits to take the 9.03 am Bristol - Bournemouth train back to the Junction Box on 20th October 1956. (S.C. Nash)

101. Ex-GWR 0–6–0 no. 3206 departs on 16th June 1962 with the 10.20 am to Evercreech Junction, the tender being on the bridge over the main road. Until 1st January 1933, the 13-lever 'B' Box was in use at this end of no. 3 platform – see map.
(E. Wilmshurst)

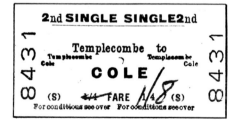

2nd SINGLE SINGLE 2nd

8431

Templecombe to
Templecombe Cole   Templecombe Cole

COLE

(S)   1/4 FARE 1/8 (S)
For conditions see over For conditions see over

8431

0152

BRITISH RAIL PLATFORM TICKET
TEMPLECOMBE
Issued to commemorate the running of
the Somerset and Dorset
Silver Jubilee Pines Express
Saturday, 5 September, 1987
Limited Edition of 500
Valid one hour. Not valid on train
5798D
(S)   For conditions see over
1 1 2 1 3 1 4 1 5 1 6

0152

WINCANTON

The old town of Wincanton is situated on the west side of Windmill Hill, at the bottom of which was the railway station and the River Cale. Two dominant features are the stone towers of the Catholic and Anglican churches, while the once imposing offices and works of Cow & Gate lay empty and neglected in 1987, as did the nearby station, 20 years earlier. The outskirts of the town are now dominated by the national road transport firm which takes its name from the town. The area around the market place retains many attractive Georgian buildings, some featuring stone mullions, as do a number of the Victorian houses. Already a modest town of over 2000 people when the railway arrived, the population increased by only about 500 by the time it closed.

102. Looking north in 1960, it is clear that barrows loaded with parcels or churns for the up platform had to be unloaded on the crossing, a potentially dangerous practice, no doubt carefully supervised by the signalman. The concrete footbridge was added by the SR during its period of responsibility for structures. It replaced an earlier lattice bridge. (R.M. Casserley)

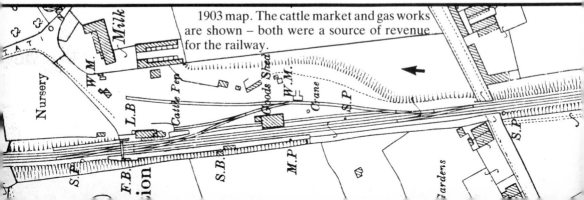

1903 map. The cattle market and gas works are shown – both were a source of revenue for the railway.

103. Unlike most of the stations on the route, Wincanton was lit by gas from the outset but, as this 1960 photograph shows, the ubiquitous SR concrete posts for electric lighting were eventually installed. Apart from over enthusiasm by the man whitewashing the platform edge, the compact stone station presented a neat appearance to the end. (R.M. Casserley)

104. In addition to the crossover in the distance, the 14-lever signal box controlled another one (behind the camera) which was removed in 1964. The two rods running to it can be seen in this 1962 view. The nameboard was white letters on a green background. (C.L. Caddy)

105. In 1933, the goods loop was extended south and two sidings run off from it to the new Cow & Gate dairy, in the left background. Class 4MT 2–6–0 no. 76026 is seen arriving with a train for Bath on 11th September 1964. The goods yard closed to general traffic on 5th April 1965.
(S.W. Baker)

347
SOM.& D.J'NT RLY. RETURN
DAY EXCURSION.
LYME REGIS to
WINCANTON
Via Templecombe
THIRD CLASS.
See over

S. & D. J't Rly.
DAY EXC'N.
WINCANTON to
LYME REGIS
Via Templecombe
THIRD CLASS.
347

0387
Somerset & Dorset Rly. Jt.C'tee.
Admit ONE MOTOR CAR
to be Parked at
WINCANTON
Station.
CHARGE 6d.
FOR CONDITIONS SEE BACK
0387

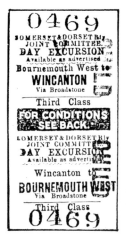

0469
SOMERSET & DORSET Rly
JOINT COMMITTEE.
DAY EXCURSION
Available as advertised
Bournemouth West to
WINCANTON
Via Broadstone
Third Class
FOR CONDITIONS
SEE BACK
SOMERSET & DORSET Rly
JOINT COMMITTEE.
DAY EXCURSION
Available as advertised
Wincanton to
BOURNEMOUTH WEST
Via Broadstone
Third Class
0469

COLE

Cole is now in effect a suburb of Bruton and is dominated by the extensive buildings of the girls school. Almost linking Cole with Bruton are the spacious grounds of Sexey's School for Boys (founded by Bishop Sexey and, amazingly, situated in the district of Lusty). The rural nature of Cole is in sharp contrast to the narrow streets of Bruton, where many of the mellow limestone buildings are used by Kings School (founded in 1516). As at Wincanton, there are two church towers but, unusually, they are both on the same church.

106. Another good example of a DCR station, Cole (for Bruton) remained uncluttered by a canopy. The company's most northerly station, it fortunately survives today, in use as a dwelling. A row of fire buckets adorn the end of the up platform shelter – these were mostly used for extinguishing cigarette ends and floating matches. (D. Cullum collection)

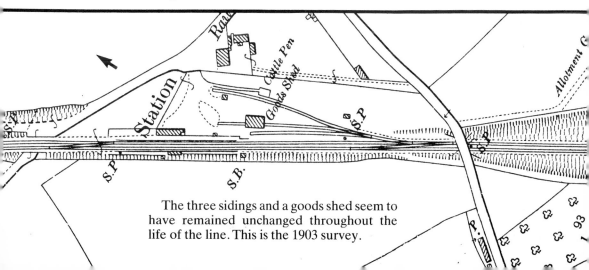

The three sidings and a goods shed seem to have remained unchanged throughout the life of the line. This is the 1903 survey.

107. Looking north in 1962, the gallows-type up starting signal is worthy of note, as is the difference in levels of the platform and the vast number of telephone wires crossing the track. The reason for this was that the pole route was on the down side of the line. The 14-lever signal box closed on 31st May 1965, as reduced train services no longer justified this block post and the goods yard had been shut in the previous month. (C.L. Caddy)

Somerset & Dorset Rly. Joint Committee

Blandford to

PRESTON

Via Bath & Birmingham.

Blandford Preston		Blandford Preston

THIRD CLASS	THIRD CLASS
Fare **36/1**	Fare **36/1**

FOR CONDITIONS SEE BACK.

0096

950C

108. In addition to the boys' schools, the nearby Sunny Hill School for Girls provided a brief period of extra traffic at the end of each term. There would have been few pupils, or indeed passengers, on 31st March 1962, as ex-GWR 0-6-0 no. 3210 waits for the guard to raise his flag, from the rear of the 2.20pm Highbridge to Templecombe service. (E. Wilmshurst)

109. Just north of Cole station, the line crossed the River Brue by means of a low five-arched viaduct, which was blown up in 1984. A little further north, this bridge was provided to take the route over the former GWR Westbury-Taunton main line. An ex-GWR 0-6-0 passes over it in 1962 – unthinkable prior to the Western Region takeover. (C.L. Caddy)

EVERCREECH JUNCTION

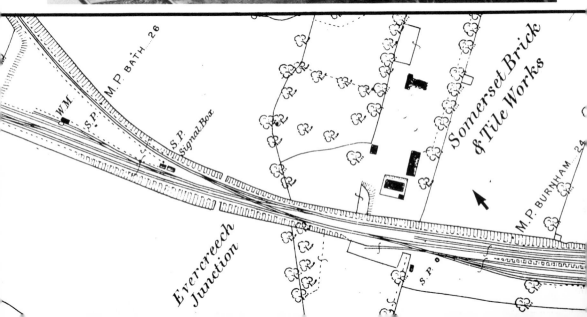

110. A station existed before the opening of the line to Bath on 20th July 1874, thereafter a new station was provided on that line, closer to the village of Evercreech. Interesting features of this early view southward include the tall lower quadrant signal, attractive oil lamps and a 6-wheeled MR van with clerestory roof. (D. Cullum collection)

Somerset& DorsetRy.JointCommittee
TOTALISATOR STAFF.
(2) Bath to (2)
0023 **WINCANTON** 0023
AND RETURN.
Third Class
13th. OCTOBER 1934
FOR CONDITIONS SEE BACK.

111. The same train is viewed from the foot-bridge and no. 17 is seen to be at its head. This was one of a batch built at the MR's Derby Works for the S&DJR. The creeper adds rural charm to the station master's house at this country junction, set amidst the fertile Somerset meadows.
(D. Cullum collection)

112. The steaming tender suggests that the fireman is damping down the coal in readiness for a tender-first departure at 8.20 am to Highbridge, with ex-MR class 4F no. 43204 on 4th August 1952. The coaches are ex-LMS compartment stock. (J.J. Smith)

The 1903 map shows a small turntable, close to the station. The three sidings on the up side were later increased to six and five were added between the diverging lines. The goods yard closed later than the others on the route, on 29th September 1965.

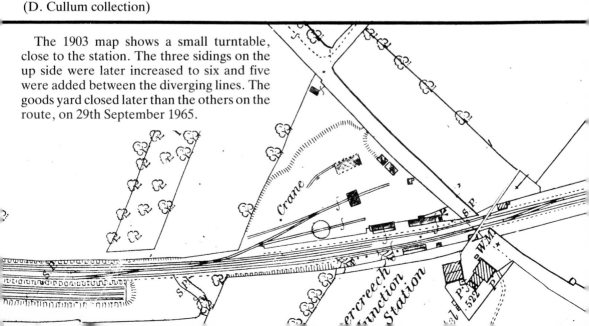

113. A view of the same train from the foot-bridge shows the smart appearance of the up platform buildings in particular. The 6.55 am from Bath is arriving behind ex-LMS class 5 no. 44839 while, in the background, the level tracks of the marshalling yard contrast with the incline of the main line. (J.J. Smith)

114. A 56ft turntable was installed in the divergence of the lines, this being large enough for class 7F 2–8–0s. Two of them are seen here on 11th September 1957 – no. 53802 on the right and no. 53808 (now preserved) on the turntable road. (P. Hay)

115. The expensive practice of double heading was reduced by the introduction of BR class 9F 2–10–0s to the line in 1960. Here we see no. 40563, the first of the LMS class 2Ps, piloting Battle of Britain class no. 34099 *Lynmouth* on 19th July 1958. The centre siding was used by pilot engines waiting to assist northbound trains over the Mendips and also to lay-over the Highbridge branch train. (S.W. Baker)

116. The last down "Pines Express" on 8th September 1962 spelt the beginning of the end for the S&D line. The last of the 9F's, *Evening Star*, takes water in the twilight of the route. While members of this class performed magnificently on the steep gradients, their use was limited as they had no equipment for steam heating the coaches in winter and were too big for the turntable, making them unavailable for freight work. (E. Wilmshurst)

117. A southward view from the footbridge on 18th May 1965 shows class 5MT 4–6–0 no. 73054 arriving with the 9.05 am from Templecombe. The base of the massive water tank can also be seen – the demand for water on a summer Saturday was enormous. (C.L. Caddy)

119. Typifying the tough individualistic character on the line and the staff who operated it, the S&DJR's own class 7F lasted nearly to the end. Originally no. 88, this engine, photographed outside Evercreech Junction goods shed, returned to steam after 18 years restoration work, a few weeks before this book was published. (S.C. Nash)

118. The undulating nature of the Somerset countryside is very evident – the Evercreech Junction water tower in the background is less so, as the Great Western Society's special departs south on 5th March 1966, just prior to closure. (J.H. Bird)

120. Although there is no longer any need to beware of trains on the S&D route, the S&D Trust have established a working museum at Washford, on the West Somerset Railway. Many relics have been restored to working order, the largest being no. 53808. (J.H. Bird)

MP *Middleton Press*

Easebourne Lane, Midhurst, West Sussex, GU29 9AZ
☎ Midhurst (073 081) 3169

BRANCH LINES
BRANCH LINES TO MIDHURST
BRANCH LINES TO HORSHAM
BRANCH LINE TO SELSEY
BRANCH LINES TO EAST GRINSTEAD
BRANCH LINES TO ALTON
BRANCH LINE TO HAYLING
BRANCH LINE TO SOUTHWOLD
BRANCH LINE TO TENTERDEN
BRANCH LINES TO NEWPORT
BRANCH LINES TO TUNBRIDGE WELLS
BRANCH LINE TO SWANAGE
BRANCH LINES AROUND GOSPORT
BRANCH LINES TO LONGMOOR
BRANCH LINES TO LYME REGIS
BRANCH LINES **AROUND** MIDHURST

SOUTH COAST RAILWAYS
BRIGHTON TO WORTHING
WORTHING TO CHICHESTER
CHICHESTER TO PORTSMOUTH
BRIGHTON TO EASTBOURNE
RYDE TO VENTNOR
EASTBOURNE TO HASTINGS
PORTSMOUTH TO SOUTHAMPTON
HASTINGS TO ASHFORD
SOUTHAMPTON TO BOURNEMOUTH

SOUTHERN MAIN LINES
WOKING TO PORTSMOUTH
HAYWARDS HEATH TO SEAFORD
EPSOM TO HORSHAM
CRAWLEY TO LITTLEHAMPTON
THREE BRIDGES TO BRIGHTON
WATERLOO TO WOKING
VICTORIA TO EAST CROYDON
TONBRIDGE TO HASTINGS

STEAMING THROUGH
STEAMING THROUGH KENT
STEAMING THROUGH EAST HANTS
STEAMING THROUGH EAST SUSSEX
STEAMING THROUGH SURREY
STEAMING THROUGH WEST SUSSEX

OTHER RAILWAY BOOKS
WAR ON THE LINE
(Reprint of the SR history in World War II)
GARRAWAY FATHER AND SON
(Biography - includes LNER, Talyllyn and Festiniog Railways)

OTHER BOOKS
MIDHURST TOWN – THEN & NOW
EAST GRINSTEAD – THEN & NOW
THE MILITARY DEFENCE OF WEST SUSSEX
WEST SUSSEX WATERWAYS
BATTLE OVER PORTSMOUTH
A City at war in 1940
SUSSEX POLICE FORCES

COUNTRY RAILWAY ROUTES
BOURNEMOUTH TO EVERCREECH JUNCTION